Plan your INVESTMENTS like an Expert

Steven Berry

foulsham

LONDON • NEW YORK • TORONTO • SYDNEY

GW00401816

foulsham

The Publishing House, Bennetts Close,
Cippenham, Berkshire, SL1 5AP, England

ISBN 0-572-02215-8

Typeset by Poole Typesetting (Wessex) Limited, Bournemouth.
Printed in Great Britain by St. Edmundsbury Press,
Bury St. Edmunds, Suffolk.

Contents

$\mathcal{I}$ntroduction

$\mathcal{T}$ he aim of this book is to provide the ordinary investor with the same tools and the same approach that professionals use when planning investment strategies. What this means is that you will be able to approach your own investments with the confidence that you are using up-to-date techniques and the same professional strategies as the experts.

The book also aims to set out all the key information and the issues that you need to understand. We demystify the whole concept of investment so that you can achieve your aims without the need for expensive and often ill-motivated advice.

The book covers investment at all stages of life, and for all amounts; from small weekly saving, to the investment of six figure sums. You should read all of the book because, even though certain parts may not apply to you at the moment, the book does have a very clearly defined central philosophy. You will help to reinforce the basic approach by applying it to the other situations outlined in the book as well as your own. You should learn how to modify and adapt the common sense approach, so that as your own circumstances change, you should be able to meet that challenge, without ever feeling that you are out of your depth.

As the book develops, you will see how to define your aims, create investment portfolios, obtain advice and information and address all the other key issues. But, most of all, in the early pages, the book demonstrates how you should always start with *you* – that is to say that *your* aims and *your* needs are of paramount importance. Don't let the availability of investments, the state of the Stock Market, the current tax regime, the motivations of the many advisers, the charges on the contract or any other important details dictate your plan. You must define your aims and stick to them. Remember, it is your money and no-one is as concerned as you about the outcome of any strategy – it is no-one else's reward, and it is no-one else's loss. So, take responsibility for your own investments and reap the rewards that a professional and expert approach should yield.

chapter 2

This chapter is intended to give you the vital elements of any investment plan. You will see immediately however, that the expert approach is not to start off with the 'Stock Market' or 'National Savings' or Risk or Taxation or any other related issues. It starts with *you* and *your* aims.

DEFINING YOUR AIMS

When you first read *Alice in Wonderland*, you probably didn't realise that it was a book on investment planning. When Alice confronts the white rabbit and discovers that he doesn't know where he is going, or when he has to get there, she concludes that it doesn't much matter whether he gets there or not. What *you* must do is ensure that in relation to your investments you know exactly where you are going and exactly when you want to arrive. Most people wouldn't dream of setting off on a holiday without a clear idea of where they were going, and the routes to get there – they would spend a little time planning. This is the key to creating your investment strategy – proper prior preparation!

WHAT ARE YOUR AIMS?

Your investment aims should be like your aims in life, because investment makes no sense in the abstract, but only where it helps you achieve stages in your life plan. Investment must be *about* something, for example, saving up for your wedding, private education for your children, or retirement. Sometimes it can be all three! So, the very first step is to sit down with your partner, if you have one, and define as clearly as possible the aims you have in life. This may be a soul searching and time consuming exercise, and you may find that there are certain disagreements between you. But, nevertheless, you must hammer out a plan on which you are both largely agreed.

It can help by dividing your aims into the *short-term* and the *long-term*. In the short-term category, you might be saving for next year's holiday, or to renew the car in two or three years' time. In the longer term category, you might be hoping to repay the mortgage on your home, or retire from work on a particular level of income. Once you have concluded what your aims are, you must commit them to memory, and to paper, so that you can continually refer to them and ensure you are on the right track.

COMPATIBILITY

You will need to define your aims by reference to the *amount* of money you need (or the amounts you have), the *risks* you are willing to take, the *timescale* over which the funds are to be invested, and the *access* you will require. So, for example, you might say 'We have five thousand pounds which we would like to double over the next seven years in order to have a fantastic holiday in Disneyland. We would like to take a reasonable amount of risk, and we don't require access to the money during the seven-year period.' That is a good example of an aim which can then be developed into the basis of investment choice.

But aims have to be tested for compatibility, so frequently one will hear people say 'I want to double my money every three years without risk and have access to it in the meantime'. This is clearly unrealistic and you and your partner must sit down and ensure that your aims make sense before you can proceed. A good financial adviser will soon be able to point out the incompatibility of your aims if you have misunderstood timescales, access, or risk. You will then have to go back to the drawing board, and the more you do this, the more refined and accurate your aims will become.

TIMESCALES

Having decided on the short- and the long-term aspects of your affairs, you can then consider what timescale you are willing to put on an investment. Some of these will be obvious, for example, retirement at 60 is clearly 30 years away when you are 30 years old. Other timescales may not be so obvious. For example, you may have children aged under ten, and decide that you would like a fund to help them through University. However, as they develop in their teens, it may be clear that one wishes to leave school at the age of 16 and may therefore need a little help financially at that stage. So, the ten-year time scale you might have set for University will need to be modified. You must take this type of contingent event into account and build in some flexibility. Therefore, a ten-year savings plan can be a very useful discipline, but if you find yourself cashing in early and suffering tremendous penalties, then it may not have been appropriate. As we develop through the book, you will see how to combine different investments to meet with unlikely, or less predictable, future events.

RISK

Clearly, there is a risk-reward model which dictates that in order to make the biggest rewards, you need to take the greatest risks. This is most obvious in gambling, where the biggest odds bring the biggest return, but also the greatest likelihood of losing your stake. This is also the case with investment, although it is not as simple as it seems. The risk-reward model is somewhat distorted and you cannot simply expect risk and reward to diverge in equal steps so that the more risk you take the more reward you can get. It doesn't always work like that. This book will discuss various distortions of which you may take advantage. For example, later in the book you will see that guaranteed equity products allow you to reap most of the reward from the Stock Market, without taking the downside risk.

ACCESS

It is absolutely no use creating an investment plan and failing to take access into account. For example, you might decide that the Stock Market, though volatile, is a good place for your savings. But, if you need them within a year, perhaps to pay off a loan, or take a holiday, then you might find the Stock Market depressed at that time and be forced into encashing at the very worst time. So, decide what access you are likely to need on what proportion of your funds, and tie them up accordingly.

BANDING

Clearly, you will have a variety of timescales, a variety of risk profiles and a variety of access requirements. This all implies a variety of approaches. You might, therefore, decide that 20 per cent of your funds need to be fairly liquid; 40 per cent tied up on a five-year view; and 40 per cent on a longer term view. Your access profile will need to match this. In this example it would be foolish to commit the whole sum to a ten-year savings plan, if you might need over half of it in the first five years!

Finally, your risk profile will probably be dictated by these timescale and access requirements. So, for short-term money you can't really afford to take risks, whereas for the ten-year plus, you can be reasonably confident of riding out the volatility of the Stock Market.

WHAT REALLY MATTERS

Staying with the basics, there are three concepts that really matter in investment and, if you remember nothing else – other than the need to define your aims – then the three issues covered in the next three sections, are at the core of successful investment strategy. They are the *real return*, the *net return* and the *income level*.

THE REAL RETURN

Many people are attracted to the high returns that seem to be offered by investment. Anything with a double digit offer seems to be good. '10 per cent income' says the advert in the Saturday press, but how much use is that? Well, the key is how the rate of return relates to the rate of inflation, and the difference between the two is the *real return*. So, for example, if a 10 per cent return is offered and inflation is 8 per cent, then you are making only a 2 per cent real return. That is to say, your money is growing by only 2 per cent in real terms, because of the eroding effect of inflation.

Conversely, if your rate of return is 7 per cent but inflation is 3 per cent, then you are actually making a 4 per cent real rate of return. What this means is that the absolute rate of return can be irrelevant.

Perhaps the best example of this is Building Society accounts. In the seventies they were offering rates of interest in the high teens, which made people very excited. Unfortunately, inflation was in the low 20 per cents, so that there was a negative real return and people became poorer and poorer every day. Their wealth actually dwindled! This is why cash can be such a bad idea.

Of late, however, bank and Building Society rates have been down to 6 per cent and 7 per cent, and the same investors have been crying into their soup. However, with inflation at 2 per cent or 3 per cent, investors are actually making a better real rate of return than they ever did when bank accounts offered 19 per cent interest!

So, never lose sight of the real rate of return, because that is what makes you wealthier. As an experiment, take a sum of £10,000 and enter it into your calculator. Then press the 'multiplication' button and press the '4', then the '%' key and then the 'plus' key. You have now compounded your money forward at a 4 per cent annual real rate of return. If you now press the 'multiplication' key, the '4', the '%' and the 'plus' keys another nine times, you have compounded your money forward 10 years. As you will see, 10 years from now, you should have £14,802; and what that means is that your money will have 40 per cent more spending power 10 years from now than it currently has if you make a relatively modest 4 per cent real return on investment. This concept of the real return is central to all investments.

THE NET RETURN

Of course, sometimes, the headline rate may not be the rate you receive. For example, 10 per cent offered by a Building Society will net down to 8 per cent after tax for most people. So, if inflation is 8.5 per cent, the headline rate is 10 per cent, and you only receive 8 per cent after tax, then you are losing one half of one percentage point on your money. So, once again, do not look at the head-line rate, but at the *net return to you.*

For example, would you rather have 10 per cent gross, or 8.5 per cent tax free? Well, clearly, 8.5 per cent tax free is better than 10 per cent for a tax payer. But this isn't the case for a non tax payer, so once again, defining your aims and knowing your own position is crucial in deciding which investment is most suitable for you.

THE INCOME LEVEL

The income level is often overlooked on investment and, it is largely a question of your position which will dictate whether or not you need income generating schemes. For example, somebody in retirement will generally need as much retirement income as they can possibly get. However, somebody in the middle stages of life with a good job should actually be saving from income and may not therefore need any income at all. Once again, it is a question of defining your aims as clearly as possible before plunging into, perhaps, unsuitable investments.

But, another issue, which is closely connected to the *net return to you* issue, is that of how you take your return. For example, there is nothing wrong with a retired person who needs a 10 per cent income, taking out a scheme that provides 10 per cent income. Nor is it inappropriate to take out a scheme that provides no income, but allows for a 10 per cent capital withdrawal. At the end of the day, you need not care – taxation matters apart – what form the money you receive actually takes. As long as you get it and your investment continues to prosper, it matters little whether it is income or capital.

CONCLUSION

So, the conclusion is this:

1 Define your aims very clearly;
2 Test those aims for compatibility;
3 Take full account of the real return;
4 Take full account of the net return;
5 Take full account of the income level.

Armed with these basic precepts, you should now be able to tackle any investment recommendation which is put to you, and start to create your own portfolio based on your clearly defined aims.

chapter 3

Creating your PORTFOLIO

INTRODUCTION

You have now defined your aims and tested them for compatibility. You have remembered what really matters, namely, the real return, the net return and the income level. So, how do you now go about selecting investments? You might have decided that a low risk, medium term, income generating asset would be appropriate, but how do you know which is which? Having clearly defined your aims, how do you select from the confusing array of financial instruments available, those which most precisely meet your requirements?

Well, the result is, thankfully, simple. You carry out your own research – and we do not mean into individual stock performance, but general reading of newspapers, books, magazines and so on – and you engage the services of those who consider themselves expert.

READING

If you read the weekend press, and perhaps one or two financial sections during the week, it will not take long before you begin to see how each investment fits into the overall scene. You will become far more familiar with the workings of unit trusts, insurance policies, warrants, options and the like, and then be more suited to discuss them. Of course, reading this book should be extremely helpful, and, to this end, we have created two tables in Appendices B and C which define the major investments in terms of risk, and in terms of their taxation treatment. You should, therefore, be able to 'invest by numbers' and simply have your plan discussed or modified by a professional, who can breathe some life into your framework.

By approaching these tables with a clear idea of your risk profile and tax position, you should get a good idea of which investments might suit you and which you should probably avoid.

THE PROFESSIONALS

There is so much advice available that it would be unwise to try to proceed without taking any. Certain investments, such as stocks and shares, yield commissions which pay stockbrokers, analysts and advisers, who may then give you their opinions. You must not take those opinions as gospel, and you must always retain a healthy scepticism, but it would be foolish not to avail yourself of some of this advice.

You must remain slightly cynical, because all this advice comes with a particular flavour. The newspapers want to write newsworthy articles and sometimes consider the facts an unnecessary distraction. Stockbrokers are unlikely to say 'we think the UK market is flat for the next three years, so don't ring us, we'll ring you'. Commission based insurance people are also likely to have a considerable amount of bias. So, ensure that you understand which way the advice is coming, and react accordingly. However, all these people can help you refine your plan.

THE RISK PYRAMID

One useful yardstick is that of the risk pyramid. Having decided your overall risk profile – and of course this may be banded as in Chapter 2 – then you should be able to create a 'stack' of investments to achieve this. The two pyramids on page 18 show a *high risk* approach and a *low risk* approach. Whilst they are not geometrically perfect, you could easily copy them by putting your own investments together and by using squared paper, would see the shape of your own pyramid. Broadly speaking, the tall narrow pyramids are higher risk than the lower broader based shapes.

IMPLEMENTATION

So, having gone through the steps of defining and testing your aims, deciding on the type of investment you require – by choosing it from the appendices at the back of this book – you then move onto implementation, the actual buying of the investments. At this stage you need to think carefully about using a professional. For example, some investments yield commissions and fees to intermediaries

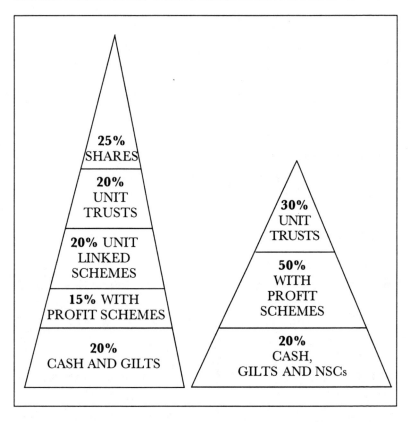

which are not available by investing directly. Accordingly, if you see a personal equity plan that you particularly like, and you send off a cheque through the post directly to the institution, you are given no credit for the commission which would otherwise be payable. By investing through an intermediary – such as a stockbroker, an insurance broker or financial planning house – a commission is generated and paid to that intermediary. You then have a business relationship with that individual whereby you might expect a degree of service in terms of providing you with valuations, advising you on fund switches and keeping you up-to-date with information on other products, even if the true motivation is to sell you more.

Many intermediaries have sophisticated computer systems on which they will record all your different assets, even if some of those, such as Building Society accounts or shares and gilts, might not have been bought through them in the first place. To have all your investments on one or two sheets of paper, and accessible at relatively short notice, is a considerable service and is generally worth the intermediary's commission or fee.

TIMING

Clearly, one of the key issues in investment is timing. For example, if you put all your funds in the market in September 1987, then it would have been a considerable time before you were back in front after the major crash of October 1987. Alternatively, had you waited until November 1987, then you would have been in profit much sooner. The real problem with investment timing is that no-one really knows what is going to happen tomorrow. Certain patterns have emerged over recent years, for example, the Stock Market generally falls or drifts in the Summer, and picks up in the last quarter of the year, more often than not. But, this type of general pattern is so easily knocked off balance by a difficult political situation, some unwelcome economic data, or a series of profit warnings from major organisations that it is hard to predict. The idea of timing, therefore, is to decide which of the investments you are considering is likely to be time sensitive.

There are two types of time sensitivity. The first one is concerned with when an investment *has* to be made. For

19

example, a personal equity plan must be made before 5 April in a particular tax year. So, if you are sitting there with your money in February and March, you are under a little bit of time pressure. The second type of time sensitivity is market driven. So if, for example, you can lock into a good interest rate when they are likely to fall, or invest in something which might be oversubscribed and have a closing date, then this will dictate the speed of your actions.

However, a word of caution. It is absolutely pointless taking out a personal equity plan for the sake of it at the end of March in a year when the market is at an all time high. It will be better for you to miss that year's entitlement and wait for a fall in the market – then again, it might not be, because the market might be rising to its next all time high! This is what makes investments unpredictable and exciting.

Secondly, if someone is trying to sell you an investment with a closing date and panic you into a rash decision, then you should back off. Very few investments are so attractive that they need to be invested in there and then, or in a very short space of time. Occasionally this is the case, but, common prudence dictates that you are better off remaining cynical and missing the odd good deal in order to avoid the disasters.

REGULAR SAVINGS

So far, we have been referring almost exclusively to capital investments. Of course, very many people do not have a capital sum and they are seeking to create one. For these people regular saving must be the answer. Of course, there is almost as much choice and a bewildering array of products for the regular saver as for the capital investor. Thankfully, the same rules apply. You must define your aims very clearly, stick to them and stick to the basics of what really matters.

For example, if you are saving up for a house deposit in the next two or three years, then you do not want stock market risk, or something where access is not available. Alternatively, if you are saving for the senior school fees of an, as yet, unborn child, then you can clearly enter a ten-year contractual commitment if the returns justify it.

The same rules apply as to real returns, net returns and risk, and the appendices at the back also point the regular saver in the right direction based on his or her risk profile and timescales.

However, there is one very interesting feature that works in the regular investor's favour and which does not always help the capital investor. This is *pound cost averaging*.

POUND COST AVERAGING

Imagine that you have a lump sum of £12,000 and that your friend has excess income of £1,000 per month. You both invest in the UK Stock Market. If the Stock Market index starts the year at 3,000 points and goes to 3,600 points, then your £12,000 will have increased by 20 per cent to £14,400. However, assuming regular investment for your friend, the result for him would be only £13,200.

Alternatively, imagine that the market begins at 3,000 points, but goes down to 2,500 points over the first six months before rising back to 3,000 over the second six months. Your £12,000 will still be worth £12,000 a year later, but the regular investor will have bought a falling Stock Market in the first six months and a rising Stock Market in the next six months, and will have paid less for all his shares than you did for yours, with a resulting fund at month 12 of £13,200. Accordingly, if a market is volatile – like the Stock Market – then regular investment can exploit this volatility by buying shares at a price which is lower than the average price throughout the term, and which is certainly lower than the initial price at the outset in this artificial example.

Regular savers can therefore do very well in such things as Unit and Investment Trust savings plans. This does not of course apply to fixed interest and cash accounts where the steady upward progression of the account will always favour the early capital investor. What it does offer, however, is a means for the small saver to have access to the Stock Market on a basis that could reduce the overall risk. Accordingly, those people saving regularly, can perhaps afford to take a slightly higher risk profile than they might otherwise have done with capital.

PHASED INVESTMENT

Of course, there is such a concept as phased investment. This means that you take your capital sum and you drip it into the market as if it were regular savings. This can be very useful if you are forced into the market as a result of timing – for example, into a personal equity plan, or as a result of capital gains reinvestment relief. You can make your investment in March – because you have to – but have that investment held in cash and dripped in over the coming months. One or two forward thinking Plan Managers offer this facility and it is very attractive at certain times. In fact, to invest both a lump sum and on a phased basis, might reduce your overall return, but does give you a useful two-way bet.

CONCLUSION

So, the steps in creating your portfolio are as follows:

1 Take your aims and run them through the appendices at the back to decide on the basic structure of your portfolio;
2 Transfer it into a pyramid to check that it conforms to the risk profile you are intending for it;
3 Engage professionals to review your strategy and ensure that, in their view, it meets your aims. This should filter out most of the wilder mistakes that might be made;
4 Choose the route through which you implement investments very carefully, so that professionals can help you and be remunerated for doing so, without it costing you any more than it would otherwise have done;
5 Consider phasing your investment when markets are high.

chapter 4

Taxation

INTRODUCTION

*Y*ou cannot invest in the UK without taking taxation into account. Even if you are not a taxpayer, many investments have tax deducted which cannot be reclaimed. If you pay any tax at all, you have to construct your investment portfolio to reflect this. If you are not a taxpayer, then it would be prudent to ensure that situation remains by planning carefully. This applies not only to income tax, but capital gains tax and, as you will see later, Inheritance Tax.

However, there is one golden rule that relates to taxation and investment – you must not let 'the tax tail wag the investment dog'. Whilst this is possibly the most appalling phrase in frequent use in investment circles, it does have a great deal of truth. What it means is that you must make an investment in the first instance because it is a good investment, and not because it brings tax benefits. It is, of course, useful to have tax benefits and enhance your return, but you must not allow them to dictate the format of your investment.

Those people who all rushed into Business Expansion Schemes in the early days gained up to 60 per cent tax relief. But as they lost all their money, it made no difference! They would have been better off in a scheme that offered no tax relief, but which gave them a good return nonetheless.

It is interesting to see how little people learn. We now have enterprise investment schemes and venture capital trusts which offer tax relief, and we have investors considering such investments, when they would normally never have done so had it not been for tax relief! If only people defined their aims clearly and stuck to them, there would be no tears shed over tax-led investments.

THE TEMPLATES

The templates in our appendices tell you precisely how each investment is taxed, based on your own tax position. You should, therefore, be able to build your portfolio whilst being fully aware of the effect taxation will have.

You will need to take differing strategies, depending upon your tax position, and this is precisely what institutions do. The investment strategy for a tax exempt pension fund is quite different from that for a taxable institution. You should apply this distinction to your own affairs. Decide where you stand on the issue of taxation, and choose the investments accordingly. Remember also, that your tax status will change from time-to-time. If you are in business, your profits may fluctuate; if you are employed you may be paying higher rates of tax now, but not paying such high rates in retirement. There is scope there for you to take out investments now, which would be liable to higher rate tax but will not mature or become taxable until you retire and become a lower rate tax payer. Planning ahead, as always, will pay dividends.

INCOME TAX

You will normally be liable to income tax on the interest element of a bank or Building Society account in the UK. You will also be taxable on the dividend yield of ordinary UK shares held in your own name. Chapter 8 on Tax Havens, will tell you how to avoid both those kinds of taxation by planning your affairs correctly.

You should also be aware that the 'capital' element of investment bonds may actually trigger an income tax liability, and you should also be aware that certain an-nuities will be taxable at only a fraction of their apparent income level.

Finally, you should be aware that you may be assessed to income tax by the withdrawal of a relief – for example, if you dispose of BES shares before the five-year period is up.

CAPITAL GAINS TAX

Capital gains tax should not be a problem for most people. In the first instance, very few people will make gains beyond the personal exempt amount of £6,300. For a husband and wife, this can mean gains of £12,600.

Added to this is indexation allowance, and this means that any gain which is really brought about by inflation, will be disregarded for the purposes of taxation. The example below sets this out. It shows that a husband and wife are able to take £41,350 from a portfolio without paying any tax at all.

Assume Assets bought in 1990 for £25,000. Current Value £41,350.	£ Tom	£ Mary
Disposal	20,675	20,675
Allowable Cost	(12,300)	(12,300)
Gross Gain	8,375	8,375
Indexation Relief ie 15 per cent of cost	(1,875)	(1,875)
Net Gain	6,500	6,500
Personal Relief	(6,500)	(6,500)
Taxable Gain	NIL	NIL

Further, by using personal equity plans, where your capital gains are all tax free, you should be able to build up an entirely tax free portfolio, which, along with sensible use of your annual exempt amount, should mean you really do not pay capital gains tax.

BED AND BREAKFASTING

The annual exemption from capital gains tax may not be carried forward to the following year. Accordingly, if you do not realise gains in a particular year, then you will not be able to use your allowance. So, if you have made gains, it is necessary for you to realise those gains by selling the shares and washing the gain out. You will be involved in the transaction costs of so doing, and perhaps a spread between prices, although this can often be negotiated.

The example below shows a portfolio which has been regularly 'Bed and Breakfasted', and one which hasn't. As you can see, the inherent gain is considerable.

Assume Tom, a 40 per cent tax payer, buys shares for £10,000 in 1986 and they increase at 15 per cent per year. By 1996 they will be worth £40,450. If they are 'bed and breakfasted' every year, the position on final disposal will be as follows, assuming £6,000 of CGT allowance pa.

	Bed & Breakfast Portfolio	Ordinary Portfolio
	£	£
Proceeds of sale	40,450	40,450
Cost	(34,380)	(10,000)
Indexation (say)	(1,000)	(5,000)
Gain	5,070	25,450
Personal Allowance	(6,000)	(6,000)
Taxable	NIL	19,450
Tax due at 40 per cent	NIL	7,780

Tom has incurred dealing costs each year but is £7,780 better off.

CAPITAL GAINS AND DEATH

They say that death and taxes go together, but this does not apply to capital gains. When the owner of an asset, which may be absolutely stuffed with capital gains, dies, then the capital gain is completely washed out. The example below shows how the new base cost for the lucky individual inheriting the asset is calculated.

Grandad Jack has a second home bought for £40,000 in 1983. It is now worth £150,000. He wants to give his son £150,000, but prefers to hold on to his cash and give the house. The year after the gift, he dies.

Giving the House

	£
Disposal 'proceeds'	150,000
Less Indexed Cost, say	(70,000)
Gain	80,000
Personal Relief	(6,500)
Taxable	73,500

Giving the Cash

If, as an alternative, Jack gives the cash then there is no CGT on 'disposal' of the cash because it is not a chargeable asset. Moreover, when Jack dies, the house will be deemed transferred at its market value of £150,000 and Jack's son will have this as his acquisition cost. He may sell the house immediately at no tax cost whatsoever. So, if you are considering making gifts, it is generally better to pass on non-chargeable assets. Mind you, you will need to consider the Inheritance Tax effects of any gifts!

INHERITANCE TAX

Many people disregard this tax because they think it will never apply to them. It is the one which replaced CTT, which replaced death duties. However, it can apply to more people than you might think. As soon as your estate reaches £215,000 then any excess may be taxed at up to 40 per cent when transferred to certain individuals, for example, your children. If you tot up the value of your home, its contents, your investments, insurance policies and so on, then, on death, it might exceed £215,000. If so, it will be reduced by tax at up to 40 per cent, and much of your investment planning will have been rendered futile.

One means to avoid this is to make a will so that your executors can see exactly how your affairs should be settled, and so that it is possible to double up for a husband and wife on the £215,000 exemption. This means only very large estates would then fall to be taxed. The tax examples at the back of the book set out different ways in which Inheritance Tax may be avoided in case study format, and you will see how easily the tax burden can be reduced, or increased, if due care is not taken.

AGE ALLOWANCE

This is a very important tax concession to the elderly. There are two special allowances for those aged 65 and 75 respectively. Such people are entitled to an extra tax allowance. However, the tax allowance is effectively means tested, and withdrawn when a certain level of income is reached. As you can see from the example below, it is possible to receive as much 'income' as you like, without restricting your age allowance. By simply re-jigging your affairs, you can save a reasonable amount of tax.

Once again, it all comes down to your sorting out precisely what your aims are, and making sure your portfolio conforms precisely with your requirements.

Assume that Bill is 68 years old and has income as follows:

	£	
Total income	16,900	
Age Allowance limit	(15,600)	
Excess	1,300 x 50% = £650 restriction	
Total income	16,900	
Personal Allowance (ie £5,220 − £650)	(4,570)	
Taxable income	12,330	
4,160 at 20 per cent	820	
8,230 at 23 per cent	1,893	
Net income	14,187	

Assume now that Money is transferred from the Building Society to National Savings Certificates:

	£	
Total income	15,600	
Personal Allowance	(5,220)	
Taxable	10,380	
3,900 at 20 per cent	820	
6,390 at 24 per cent	1,444	
Net income	13,336	
Plus 'return' from NSCs	1,300	
Total effective income	14,636	Saving £449

CONCLUSION

You cannot ignore taxation and it should be an important factor in the creation of your portfolio. However, do not let it dictate the portfolio's shape. In summary, you should:

1 Take advantage of all the allowances available. For example, the capital gains exempt limit and Personal Equity plans;
2 Make sure that your investments suit your tax position precisely. For example, with age allowance;
3 Study in depth the tax saving strategies and case studies at the back of the book.

chapter 5

Specific INVESTMENTS

This section looks at investments in detail one by one, considering their tax treatment, risk profile, likely return and access. It is relatively exhaustive and should be used in conjunction with the templates at the back of the book. Once you have studied this section, you should have a very clear idea of how various different investments work. Moreover, you should be able to select from this list those investments which most accurately meet the aims you have set out. It may be, that having considered what is available, your aims require a little modification. If this is the case, don't worry, it is quite natural and desirable for your aims to go through a period of gradual and continued modification in order to hone them to perfection.

LOWER RISK INVESTMENTS

INTRODUCTION

There is an attractive array of lower risk investments which allows individuals and institutions to fine tune their portfolios and their risk profiles.

CASH

Cash is not really an investment, but is a useful safe haven. For example, one of the most important principles of investment is knowing when not to invest, or when to take a profit and sit on that profit for a while before re-investing. When this strategy is required, then cash is the only viable option. At times like this, you will need to decide whether you want a simple cash account, such as that with a bank or Building Society – with relatively good access, so that you can deal quickly in the market – or whether you are out of the market for a sustained period during which you will be able to accept a longer timescale on the investment, say 30 or 90 days. You might also like to consider whether or not gross interest would be in your favour, for example, in an off-shore bank account.

The reason that cash is not really an investment is that it rarely produces a real rate of return. At the beginning of 1996, interest rates were around 6–7 per cent, whilst inflation was 2–3 per cent. This meant that cash was producing a healthy real rate of return, even after taxation and various charges. However, over the longer term, this would not usually be the case and it would be unlikely to remain so. But there is nothing wrong with your holding cash as an investment whilst it is producing a satisfactory real return and on the grounds that it is so liquid and allows you to move quickly should you need to.

Finally, cash may be useful so that you can pay the charges on a managed portfolio – ie one where a discretionary manager is managing your investment for a fee – or meet such things as Rights Issues and so on, without the need for selling investments, which could be inconvenient.

GILTS/BONDS

Gilts and Bonds are misunderstood. Whilst gilts are guaranteed by the British Government and therefore have a very low risk profile, this does not mean that their price fluctuations will be similarly risk free. For example, if interest rates are 5 per cent, and a gilt is trading at its par value, then when interest rates go to 10 per cent, the par value of the gilt will fall very considerably, because it is only providing half the income it should. Similarly, if you have a 10 per cent gilt trading at par, and interest rates fall to 5 per cent, then a significant tax free capital gain may be made. This is because the gilt is then providing twice the income that the market provides and therefore the capital value is notionally twice as great, although there are other distortions and limiting factors. In times of interest rate volatility therefore, gilts can carry a serious risk of capital loss.

Bonds which are issued by large companies or local authorities often have wilder fluctuations, because there is a greater degree of risk. Clearly, a local authority is far less safe than the Government itself. In this case, the interest rate which those bonds pay will be higher to reflect the added credit risk. Because the coupon is entirely taxable, you will need to take this into account when judging the

35

basic net return to the investor. Similarly, you would be ill advised generally to buy such bonds at a time of low interest rates because you will probably be paying over par. As the interest rates rise in the cycle, the capital value of your investment may fall. So, even though these investments are low risk, they still carry the risk of capital fluctuations.

NATIONAL SAVINGS CERTIFICATES

National Savings Certificates have certain advantages to the individual holder. For example, the freedom from tax of most issues means that at a time of high taxation the real gross return is much higher. For example, if the return on the next issue of saving certificates were 7.5 per cent, then this would be worth nearly 10 per cent to the basic rate tax payer, but 12.5 per cent to the higher rate tax payer, in gross terms. The higher rate tax payer would therefore need a consistent five-year interest rate of 12.5 per cent from another investment in order to compare.

Additionally, there are index linked certificates which link their return directly to the rise in prices and guarantee to outperform that rise. Accordingly, you are guaranteed a real rate of return.

The downside of these investments is that access is always a problem. In the case of most five-year certificates, they must be allowed to run their course before you can encash them. This may be inconvenient if interest rates rise. For example, imagine you buy savings certificates which pay a net 5 per cent, when interest rates are a gross 5 per cent. You will be happy with your net return because it exceeds the prevailing net interest rate by some 2 per cent and therefore is an attractive real rate of return. But, if interest rates rise to, say, 7 per cent or 8 per cent, then you will be locked into a potentially unattractive investment. It is this lack of access that makes some National Savings products unattractive for certain purposes.

WITH PROFIT POLICIES

Insurance companies issue with profit policies which give a certain basic guarantee of, say, 4 per cent to any funds invested. Each year they add a further 'reversionary bonus' and this enhances the investment still further. It is notable that such bonuses, once declared, cannot be removed and so the value of such policies increases over time. Moreover, on death, on the maturity or the encashment of a policy there may be a further terminal bonus to enhance the investment still further.

The problem with these policies in the past was that they always had to be accessed via a regular premium scheme, and this carried with it all the constraints and inflexibility of a 10, 20 or 25 year policy. However, over recent years, single premium schemes have been available and whilst they have penalties in, say, the first five years, from year five onwards, you should be able to access your funds and in any event, most life companies will pay you an income in the meantime. Accordingly, such investments can be very attractive if you are happy, effectively, to lock away your money for, say, five years and allow the vague behaviour of the life company actuary declaring bonuses, to determine the value of your investment. You should note that bonuses are liable to fluctuate and are at the discretion of the life company actuary.

With Profit Bonds have certain important taxation advantages in that basic rate taxation is deemed already to have been deducted. What this means is that the return is effectively 'tax free' for a basic rate tax payer and a higher rate tax payer will need pay only the difference between the higher rate and the basic rate on encashment. In 1996, this currently means a tax rate of some 16 per cent.

Most investors will, undoubtedly, consider the planning opportunities which such bonds offer. For example, higher rate tax payers could buy their schemes without ever taking income until such time as they are a basic rate tax payer perhaps in retirement. This would, effectively, have been a very good shelter during years of high taxation only to provide tax free returns when the income is needed. Moreover, business losses, or pension payments which reduce the amount of tax paid, will all have an effect in assisting the tax planning side of bond ownership.

PENSIONS

It is worth pausing for a moment to consider the whole subject of pensions. Whilst the risk profile of the pension scheme may be altered by choosing the fund links and assets within it, so that it can be anything from, almost nil, to very high risk, it is worth considering at this stage, because pensions provide such an important part of many people's overall investment strategy.

Whether a pension is a personal pension or a company scheme, it should carry the same tax benefits which are very significant. Firstly, all qualifying contributions will be completely allowable for income tax and this means relief at up to 40 per cent. Secondly, whilst the pension funds are growing, they will be completely free of tax, so that the accumulated wealth builds up much more quickly. Thirdly, on retirement there is generally the option to have a completely tax free lump sum and in some cases this can be almost all the pension fund. Finally, should you die whilst you have money invested in a pension fund, it can be paid to your nominated beneficiaries without any inheritance tax.

So, pensions are really a very useful, highly accessible tax haven, available to almost all people and capable of being tuned to suit a variety of different risk profiles.

Chapter 8 gives an example of how funds can increase very dramatically inside a pension scheme, as opposed to outside.

However, outside of the compelling tax reasons for investing in a pension scheme, there are other advantages. Firstly, you cannot generally get at your money until you are at least 50, which prevents your frittering it away if you are not a very disciplined saver. Secondly, you can use a pension fund to support a mortgage, planning that your future tax free cash will pay off the loan from your Building Society or bank. In the meantime, you will be accruing a very useful pension income.

Finally, investment in pensions is available from a very low base, usually as little as £25 a month, although you should be wary of how much charges will eat into small amounts. Pensions then offer a very tax efficient means of increasing wealth and are useful for nearly all savers, with the exception of those who are already retired. They can be simple or very sophisticated and should form a core element of your saving programme.

MEDIUM RISK INVESTMENTS

INTRODUCTION

Medium risk investments are popular with a great many people. Whether this is because they meet most people's expectations of risk and reward, or whether it is a great British passion for compromise, the fact remains that the investments considered in this section are likely to be the bulk of an individual's portfolio.

UNIT TRUSTS

Unit Trusts are simply pooled funds which allow individual investors access to a wide range of investments throughout the world and to professional expertise, but on a very much reduced basis. For example, to have a portfolio actively managed and spread throughout the world would probably require an initial investment of seven figures. However, a Unit Trust may offer this from as little as £1,000. Whilst the charges can be fairly stiff, for example, 5 per cent or 6 per cent on the way in, and 1 per cent annual management charge, because of booming stock markets over recent years, the net return to investors has been very attractive.

In terms of access, the funds can generally be obtained with only a few days delay. The exception to this is in times of exceptional economic turmoil when Unit Trust groups reserve the right to refuse redemption of certain types of unit, or to alter the price significantly.

From a taxation viewpoint, Unit Trusts can be attractive to the private investor because they are chargeable assets for the purposes of capital gains tax. This means that if they are sold and there is a gain, this will be chargeable to capital gains tax. As each individual has an exemption of £6,500, this means that he or she can effectively take this amount of gain every year tax free.

The income tax side is less easy to avoid because dividends are paid with basic rate deducted and non tax payers will reclaim it, whereas higher rate tax payers will pay a little extra. You can decide to buy low yielding Unit Trusts where the amount of income is small or negligible. There are many funds available with a yield of only a fraction of 1 per cent. One common misconception, however, is that 'accumulation units', instead of 'income units', are tax free. This is not the case – they simply function by rolling up any net income and leaving you to settle the tax liability, tax reclaim or further tax liability, as applicable.

Despite this small tax drawback, Unit Trusts can be particularly useful for individuals, especially when they want to obtain access to overseas markets in a small or controlled way.

In terms of risk, whilst Unit Trusts spread the risk by having a wide range of shares and therefore diluting the effect of any single share going bust, you can more or less decide on the risk profile you want with an almost infinite variety. For example, if you were to choose UK Unit Trusts, or those which simply track the index in the UK Stock Market, then you are more or less guaranteed to follow the market and benefit from its gains or falls – after management charges of course. Conversely, by investing in South East Asian, other One-Market or Emerging Market funds, Technology stocks or smaller companies, you can significantly increase your risk profile.

From this point of view then, Unit Trusts probably straddle the whole risk profile from low/medium risk to medium/high risk. This is what makes them so popular and the whole UK Unit Trust market is worth £1,000 Million.

CORPORATE BONDS

In the low risk section we discussed Gilts and First Class Paper – ie bonds issued by major institutions or foreign countries. In the medium risk section, bonds would still appear, but would be represented by those issued by less worthy organisations, such as countries with a history of default on debt, or those issued by stocks that are not as strong as the FT 100. Moreover, there are Eurobonds denominated in foreign currencies where you are effectively taking a currency risk at the same time as an investment risk. For example, if you take a 10 per cent bond in Deutschmarks, but Deutschmarks depreciate by 50 per cent against the pound, you will find yourself with a halved income and halved capital. Whilst this is extreme and unlikely, the point should still be understood. You can rack up the risk profile of a bond by denominating it a foreign currency.

UNIT LINKED LIFE POLICIES

The with-profit policies referred to in the Low Risk section offered guarantees. Unit linked policies offer no such guarantees generally, and you are therefore subject to the expertise, or otherwise, of the managing institution. Most life assurance companies provide a wide range of funds from the mixed and managed, through to the single country funds and specialised market funds. They allow you to access them on a monthly basis through insurance policies and in a very small way. You might, for example, pay £50 a month into a unit linked savings plan and divide the contribution into ten funds. You therefore have approximately £5 going into each fund each month; which means that over a year you would only have invested some £60 in your Far Eastern fund and so on! Nonetheless, over time, you should benefit from the rises and falls in these markets and a taxation treatment of such life policies.

Any life policy held for ten years, or three quarters of the term, if shorter, should generally be entirely free of tax. Whilst it is true that the sponsoring life assurance company will pay corporation tax on its underlying investments, the fact that the overall return is completely free of tax could be most advantageous to a higher rate tax payer. Not only that, but life companies can play a clever game of offsetting the expenses of new business acquisitions against their tax liability so that their effective tax rate may be in the low teens.

The real problem is access. It is very difficult to obtain your funds from a long term life assurance contract without some significant penalties. For example, it may be that after two or three years in such a policy, the amount returned to you is a fraction of what you paid in, let alone any growth. However, if you can live with the inflexibility, and fund the scheme for the original intended term, then you should be able to reap the benefits of the tax freedom. Once again it is a balancing act.

GUARANTEED EQUITY FUNDS

Earlier on, we mentioned various distortions of the risk reward equation. Guaranteed equity funds are just such a distortion.

These funds work by giving you a basic guarantee that your capital will not be lost. At the end of a predetermined period, say five years, you are guaranteed to get back at least what you put in. In the meantime, your funds are exposed to the full rise in the Stock Market index, or several different indices. What this means is that if there is some sort of terrible crash, you will not lose your money, even though you have been in the market. If the market roars ahead, then you will do very well.

The major drawback with these funds is that you do not get dividend income, as this is used by the fund issuers in order to provide the guarantees, which are effectively re-insured through options and other derivative contracts. Moreover, being guaranteed your money back in five years time is not spectacular because you have lost five years interest or growth. Nevertheless, for the cautious investor, this can be a sensible way to invest in the Stock Market without fear of being wiped out.

More recently, annual funds, or even quarterly funds have become available. Moreover, you can choose the amount of capital guarantee you want, and this affects the amount of Stock Market growth you get. You might, for example, decide that you want 105 per cent of your money returned at the end of one year so that you have definitely made something. The downside would be that you would then get only 75 per cent of the rise in the Stock Market. But, this is a gamble that might suit some people.

Far more interesting however, is the approach whereby you guarantee only 90 per cent of your capital but your participation rate in Stock Market rises goes up to 300 or so per cent. As such a strategy is available quarterly, you can actually have a three-fold participation in Stock Market rises, but a maximum loss per quarter of 10 per cent. If you run this through, say, the last ten years, then the gains you could have made are truly phenomenal.

This is a market, more than any, where you will need professional advice. For example, some Building Societies and Life Companies are still pedalling 95 per cent capital guarantees and 75 per cent participation. As you can get 100 per cent participation at the same guarantee, or 100 per cent guarantee on the same participation, you really can make a professional earn his or her fee by choosing the best scheme for you.

TRACKER FUNDS

This is another way to control your risk in investment. A tracker fund simply replicates the relevant index, say, for example, the FT 100. If a stock moves out of the FT 100 and a new one replaces it, then the tracker fund will act accordingly, buying and selling, to balance its books. What this means is that you can follow the index, if it rises, your fund will rise, but if it falls, your fund will fall. As the general trend of the index over any reasonable period is to rise, you more or less guarantee yourself some growth. However, because of dealing costs and other fund management charges, you will always lag behind the index a little bit. Although, with up to 80 per cent of fund managers failing to beat the index, you at least save yourself from the potential disaster of choosing a very bad fund manager who halves your money and halves it again. It is for this reason that 'passive investment' has become popular. However, the geared guaranteed equity funds described above probably represent a better option.

PREMIUM BONDS

This is a difficult investment to classify and some would not consider it an investment at all. However, it has been calculated that an investment of £10,000 per head in Premium Bonds should, over time, produce a 7 per cent net return. To a higher rate tax payer, this would be worth 11.67 per cent and so may be attractive. Of course, whilst there is the major upside of a very significant win, you cannot guarantee any return at all and you could go year-after-year-after-year gradually eroding the value of your capital. It is for this reason that the investment, if

45

it can be classified at all, should be considered low to medium risk.

HIGHER RISK INVESTMENTS

INTRODUCTION

People are often attracted to higher risk investments because there is a degree of excitement. Sitting at the golf club professing to owning a broadly based Unit Trust does not have the same cachet as claiming to be a derivatives trader and 'straddling the iron horse' in the traded options market. However, this is an area where warnings are most required. It is so easy for the private investor to come a cropper with higher risk investments. Whilst the risk profile is the same for everybody in the abstract, in relative terms, those with an expert knowledge of the market, more experience, more research and more inside information, will generally be able to control their higher risk investments much more easily. So, do be extremely careful when deciding how much of your portfolio is going to be angled to the higher risk side.

UNIT TRUSTS

Unit Trusts are included as high risk investments for the reasons stated above; namely, that you can tune the risk profile quite considerably. Moreover, you can invest in foreign countries, which means that somewhere along the line there will probably be a foreign currency play which can also make life difficult. The number of people who are mystified when their US Unit Trusts do not go up in price despite the market in the States rising and fail to understand it is because the dollar is also rising – or falling, if the fund is incorrectly hedged against currencies – is one of the biggest problems in managing diversified international portfolios.

INVESTMENT TRUSTS

Investment trusts must not be confused with Unit Trusts. Unit Trusts are simply open ended pools of funds intended to be invested in a broadly based fashion. Investment trusts are, however, single companies with a set capital structure which is not open ended. They are bought and sold on the Stock Exchange and therefore are subject to sentiment more directly than a Unit Trust. Moreover, they are allowed to borrow to fund their investments and this introduces a further element of risk.

Finally, although there are some very broadly based international funds, which do seek to reduce their overall risk, there is also a considerable number of very specific funds which invest in particular areas, such as technology or computing. Clearly, such funds will be far more subject to fashion and trends in investment and hence a little riskier.

INDIVIDUAL SHARES

Many people fail to see the risk of individual shares. Isn't Marks & Spencer in every High Street? Don't they have a turnover which is now fed from all over the world? Well of course they do. However, it should also be understood that, as an individual stock, they could be the subject of a hostile takeover, or a loss of their management team, or a few unhappy diversifications, say, into financial services, mobile telephones or house building. The complexion of

47

a share and the market's view of it can change very dramatically overnight. Just look at the utilities and how some have doubled and doubled again, whilst others have halved, due to monopolies investigations.

It is worthwhile noting that when Pollypeck went bust, investors who held the share lost the vast majority of their value. However, holders of the Fidelity UK Special Situations Trust which held the share, saw the price fall by only one half of one per cent. So, individual stocks are risky, although the FTSE constituents are generally less risky than the second and third line stocks.

WOODLANDS

It is possible to invest in forestry and gain certain tax breaks. For example, owning woodlands is treated as a business for Inheritance Tax purposes and so you might get an effective 40 per cent discount on your wealth. Moreover, you can roll-over certain capital gains and therefore use woodlands as a shelter. However, you need to be very wealthy before direct investment in forestry can yield any real advantages and you will certainly need specialist advice. For the vast majority of investors, it would be well worth avoiding.

CURRENCY FUNDS

With the emphasis on Europe, currency funds have received a great deal of attention. The European Monetary Union focused investors' minds on the gains to be made in currency markets. For example, if there were four Deutschmarks to the pound in 1980 and there are now only two and a half, then by leaving your funds in Deutschmarks throughout that period, you would have increased your sterling equivalent holding by 60 per cent. However, in the meantime, you would have suffered lower rates of interest from your German bank account than you would have received from your UK bank account, so you do need to look at the total net return to the investor.

Similarly, there might be a currency which is offering a 10 per cent rate of interest, when UK rates are only, say 6–7 per cent. However, if the currency depreciates markedly whilst you are investing, then you will lose capital although you have made income and your overall net return may be no better.

Recognising that opportunities do, nevertheless, exist, but that individual investors find it hard to deal in the markets with any speed and indeed without the costs cancelling out much of the gain, many fund managers have started to offer currency funds.

On the one hand, there are single currency funds, denominated in, say, yen, or US Dollars. This allows individuals to make a play on a particular currency and its likely future strength against sterling.

Other managed funds exist, confining themselves to six or seven major currencies and where the managers are supposed to be able to be in the right currency at the right time.

Currency markets are as volatile as Stock Markets and the returns to be made often lag behind a good equity fund. There can be occasions when investment in currency funds can be appropriate, for example, where you have liabilities denominated in a particular currency, it might be wise to hold that currency so that your assets do not move out of equilibrium to your liabilities. For example, imagine you have a mortgage of £60,000 in sterling and have

£60,000 of savings. If you go to work in Japan, you would be wise to keep £60,000 in sterling so that no matter what happens to sterling against the yen, you will still be able to pay off your loan. If you convert to yen, and the yen depreciates by, say 50 per cent, then when you convert back, you will have only £30,000 and not be able to pay off your loan.

In investment terms however, currency funds are rather specialised and for the more sophisticated and wealthy investor.

WILD INVESTMENTS

INTRODUCTION

Until recent years, I used to class these investments as higher risk, but I think that a new category is needed because of the phenomenal gearing and speed of action which global markets have brought about.

PENNY SHARES

It is extremely attractive to buy a share for two or three pence and sell it for a pound. We all know this, but the number of people who have done this successfully is very small. Moreover, the number who have done it successfully repeatedly and whose overall portfolio of Penny Shares shows a profit, are few and far between.

The point about Penny Shares is that the market is very small and it is quite possible that a few purchases will move the price. For example, imagine a share is written up in a cheap Share Guide which hits people's doormats at the weekend and is also mentioned in one or two quality newspapers. The share stands at two or three pence and in fly the punters on Monday morning. By the afternoon, the share may have doubled in value, so the punters now think they are right and double up again. By Tuesday afternoon the share is ten pence, when, lo and behold, all the boys who bought it prior to the production of the Share Guide and tips in the paper, all sell out at eight, nine or ten pence and the share price collapses back to the two pence, which is what the share is fundamentally worth. This may sound like a rather cynical outlook, but Penny Shares are volatile and not at all reliable. Generally speaking, apart from the excitement value, there is little to be gained by putting your portfolio in such unreliable shares.

STOCK MARKET WARRANTS

Most investors will come across warrants if they buy investment trusts. Warrants give you the right – although you are not obliged to exercise it – to buy an ordinary share at a particular price on a particular future date. In the meantime, the warrants can be bought and sold.

Because the warrant price will always be a fraction of the share price, you can get quite a dramatic return. For example, if a warrant costs you 10 pence and allows you to buy a share for £1, and that share currently stands at £1.10, you will be cost neutral. If the share goes to £1.20 then you can buy it for £1, sell it for £1.20 and you have, effectively, doubled your 10 pence stake. So, a very small movement in a share price can have a dramatic effect on the warrant.

Of course, there is very limited information available on warrants and the market is very narrow, so it can be very difficult to deal. In the meantime, you get no rights to dividends and you probably cannot vote. Not only that, the gearing works both ways and the money can literally be wiped out almost overnight.

OPTIONS, FUTURES, DERIVATIVES

The market for derivatives is extremely complicated and subject to wild fluctuations in minutes. Those who endeavour to make money, do so by trading on a twenty-four hour basis, with every piece of information at their finger tips. It stands to reason therefore that most private investors will be severely disadvantaged by trying to keep up with such a market. This does not mean that you cannot do well, but it means that the chances of your being successful are pretty remote.

Firstly, for every option that you buy, there is a seller on the other end. The odds are that this fellow is far more sophisticated and has a greater knowledge of the likely movement in a particular stock. Accordingly, you are on a hiding to nothing when you begin and most traded options expire worthless. Accordingly, you would be well advised to limit this sort of activity to a fraction of your portfolio, say, no more than 5 per cent.

For those people who are serious about derivative contracts, Appendix D details two trading strategies which will limit your exposure and allow you to participate without too great a risk. However, the greatest wealth warning must be added to any section discussing traded options or other derivatives.

OPTIONS AND GEARING

Whilst it is unlikely that most investors will find options suitable, you should at least understand how they work and the gearing involved, so that when investing in individual companies, you can assess their financial health by asking them whether or not they use derivatives in their treasury division.

Take the example of an option in ABC Ltd, whose price is £3 a share in June. If you think the price will rise to £4 over the next six months, you might want to invest, but you might not have all the money. You therefore buy a 'ABC Ltd £3 December Call'. Imagine that the price of this is 10 pence. If the shares rise above £3.10, you are 'in the money', which means that you can exercise your option, buy the shares for £3, you have spent £3.10 in total and you are cost neutral.

However, if the shares rise to £3.50, you can exercise your option at £3 and sell immediately, making 50 pence profit. You have now made 40 pence on your 10 pence stake, a gain of 400 per cent! Even though the shares rose by only 50 pence, or 16.6 per cent, you made 400 per cent. The downside of course is that if the shares do not move in the right direction within the set timescale, all your money will be lost. From this point of view, options are rather like gambling and are most unlikely to suit the majority of people.

UNUSUAL INVESTMENTS

Over the years there have been times when unusual investments have yielded a very good return. For example, coins or antiques may well provide you with the opportunity to make a significant amount of money. I knew a chap who use to buy violins and made tens of thousands of pounds because his expert knowledge was rare, and he was able to apply it with due prudence.

53

However, the classic car boom is a perfect example of how vicious a market can be. In the early 1980s, people would abandon Aston Martins on the street, rather than fix them and they could be bought for as little as £2,000. However, the boom began and prices started to climb so that £25,000 might be the entry level. Soon, it was up higher than this, only to sustain itself for a short period before collapsing back down, although not as far as the original starting point. In any event, the people who paid £5,000 well before there was any boom were probably genuine enthusiasts who had no intention of selling and who therefore probably didn't. It would have been a long sighted investor indeed who predicted this particular phenomenon.

Of course, there is often another justification for having unusual investments and that is that they may be enjoyed in themselves. I know many people who buy cases of fine wine and, over the years, the one bottle can pay for the entire case. The worst result is that a proportion of the case, or cases, may be held back but they are then 'free' and there is a degree of satisfaction in that alone.

Of course, the market is fickle and whilst values may fluctuate wildly, there are other attendant problems, such as storage and insurance, for collections of anything valuable or bulky. The advice here then is that if you have a particular interest, do not turn it into investment per se, but simply enjoy the interest for what it is and, if you make money – fine – but if you don't, it will simply be a secondary issue of little importance.

Finally, a word on trading. If the Inland Revenue think that you are carrying out an activity as a hobby, then they will be likely to leave you alone. But, if you begin trading, and there are several important tests which are applied to see whether or not you are trading (see Appendix E), then they will be within their rights to tax you on any profits you make. Far better to keep it as a hobby and take your gains tax free, but, more likely, in the pleasure of ownership and use or consumption.

CONCLUSION

There is clearly a very wide range of risk profiles available by selecting your investments carefully. You will also need to be careful because some investments, such as pensions or unit trusts, can go from low risk, such as the cash or gilt funds, through to much higher risk, such as geared funds or currency funds.

So, the steps you should take are as follows:

1   Define your investment aims clearly;
2   Take them through the matrix, (see Appendix C) to highlight possible investments;
3   Create your own portfolio from these results;
4   Take this portfolio to one of your advisers to see how it should be finely tuned;
5   Implement the recommendations through those advisers when appropriate in order to offset their fees with commissions available.

chapter 6

Case STUDIES

INTRODUCTION

*M*any people find it more comprehensible if they can see investments working in practice, not just in their own circumstances, but in a variety of other circumstances. This section sets out various case studies which show how investments may come together at different times of life in order to achieve an individual's or his family's aims. Whilst the examples below try to extract as many general principles as possible, it should be appreciated that your own situation will be unique and that you will need to carry out the exercise of defining your aims in detail before you can really benefit from these case studies.

YOUNG SINGLE PERSON AGED UNDER 25

Let us assume that this individual has no dependents, is living at home and is in full employment. Whilst it would be tempting to spend every penny of income, as soon as saving begins the better. For example, £100 per month saved for 30 years will be worth twice as much as £200 saved for 15 years. This is a staggering statistic in itself and should make younger people consider the cost of delay in investment.

Specific Investments

Clearly a TESSA would be useful because it offers a very low risk real rate of return which is also very tax efficient. It can be funded from income from as little as £20 per month and is likely to establish a savings habit which may last a lifetime. Moreover, if a bank or Building Society provides the TESSA, they may well be the first port of call for a mortgage in later years.

If there is excess savings capacity available after the TESSA, then personal equity plans may be considered. A nice low risk investment into, say, a broadly based tracker fund will allow an individual to participate in the Stock Market at greatly reduced risk and cost.

Clearly, there is no real need for life assurance so long as there is someone around to bury the individual in the, hopefully, unlikely event that he or she dies. However, it would be prudent to be in a pension scheme from two viewpoints. On the one hand, there is the cost of delay mentioned above, and the disproportionate effect of early contributions. On the other hand, there is the point that a pension would then be kicked off under existing legislation which is likely to be better than that which follows.

57

If, for some reason, legislation becomes easier, then a second pension can be started under the new rules. So, it is well worth securing a contract even with a minimum contribution, particularly when you consider the generous tax benefits surrounding pensions.

Of course, some young people have capital to invest and this needs to be the core of a flexible future portfolio. The table below shows how £20,000 might be invested for an individual who is taking a five-year view before they need to buy a home.

£3,000 – TESSA
£6,000 – Personal Equity Plan
£5,000 – Index Linked National Savings Certificates
£3,000 – Unit Trusts
£3,000 – Pensions
_____
£20,000
_____

The portfolio above has a reasonable mix between low and medium risk, exploits various tax reliefs available and has a reasonable degree of access. It is a good compromise portfolio for the majority of people in this category.

MARRIED WITH CHILDREN

At this stage, a mortgage will normally have been obtained and a family home may be in the process of being bought. It probably means there is little left for active saving, particularly if there are children. Well, and this is one of the most difficult aspects of investing from income, it is important to balance today with tomorrow and realise that your earnings will need to be spread throughout your entire life and not just your working life. Accordingly, you should keep the saving habit as long as you can and flexible investments such as cash, TESSAs or low risk PEPs, may be the only practical answer.

What will also be of paramount importance is some sort of life assurance contract to replace your income in the event of your death. Investment is largely about responsibilities to yourself, and you should also cover the responsibilities you have to other people.

What is often left unsaid is that investments can of course be sold and re-applied. So, in this case it would be quite legitimate to allow the TESSA and the Index Linked Savings Certificates to mature and cash in the PEP in order to provide a deposit for a first home. This is what investment is about, saving for a known commitment, and there is no unwritten law that says once an investment is bought it must be kept for ever.

MIDDLE YEARS

This section follows on from the previous one on the assumption that investments have been sold and re-applied and that the major expenditure now is on children approaching their teens and the funding of a mortgage sufficient to buy a family home.

At this stage, individuals should continue to emphasise life assurance requirements and take every opportunity to join any available pension scheme, particularly if there is an employer contribution. Even if self-employed, individuals will need to consider pensions, so that the disproportionately successful earlier years may have full effect.

Remember, £100 per month for 20 years will be worth far more than £200 per month for 10 years!

It should be possible to plan for the major expenditure required, for example, any school fees or help with University education or deposits on houses. For these purposes, TESSAs and National Savings will still be appropriate at the lower risk end and unit and investment trusts at the higher risk end. If tax shelters are available, they should be used. The portfolio below shows how capital and income might be invested:

£5,000 – Unit/Investment Trust PEP
£3,000 – TESSA
Balance to pensions and life assurance.

If more income is available, then the PEP should be maximised.

LATER YEARS

At this stage, all the children should have matured and be reasonably independent. Investment priorities will probably be catching up on pension contributions and other investment issues which have been shelved, given the need to spend on the children, cover life assurance requirements and possibly provide capital for education.

It should be the first time for years that there is genuine surplus income and whilst such things as TESSAs and PEPs should still be funded, additional voluntary contributions to occupational pension schemes, or increased funding to self-employed pension schemes will probably be a priority. Given that the family home may well be on its way to being paid for, if there is a repayment mortgage in place, or there will be considerable value in an endowment or other repayment method, then life assurance may be less important. The chief aim will probably now be working towards a definite retirement date and the portfolio below might be appropriate:

£ 9,000 – TESSA
£11,000 – Unit Trust PEPs
£ 2,000 – Increased Pension Funding
£ 5,000 – Indexed-linked NSCs
£ 3,000 – Emergency cash fund

£30,000

IN RETIREMENT

Now that the individuals have retired, the main requirement has to be income and an income which will hold its own against inflation. As previously stated, it is only the net return to the investor that matters, so 'income' may come in the form of surrendered capital as long as there is no unplanned erosion of that capital.

Once again, the staple elements of TESSAs and broadly based PEPs will be present to provide real rates of return and a reasonably tax efficient income. National Savings will be suitable and an emergency cash fund will also be wise. However, increased capital due to having taken a tax free cash sum will need to be invested in a variety of ways. With-profit insurance bonds will provide a useful low-risk holding and gilts may also be appropriate providing a reliable income. Of course, the portfolio will need to be constructed with age allowance in mind, but the example below should be a good starting point.

£ 9,000 – TESSA
£21,000 – UT PEPs
£10,000 – Gilts
£ 5,000 – Indexed linked NSCs
£ 3,000 – Cash fund
£10,000 – Non-PEP Unit and Investment Trust
£20,000 – With profit bond
£12,000 – Single company PEPs

£90,000

The portfolios above act only as pointers and each individual, couple or family, will have different priorities. For example, a civil servant with an index linked non-contributory pension scheme and a good death in service benefit, may be able to direct more funds towards unit and investment Trusts or PEPs.

Conversely, a self-employed individual will need to look at life assurance and pensions very seriously before addressing TESSAs, PEPs and so on. However, it should be clear how the various components of abstract investment go together in order to create a portfolio.

chapter 7
Other important ISSUES

INTRODUCTION

have tried to define the major, important and timeless principles of investment, such as defining your aims, looking at a real return and examining the net return to the investor. Once you have taken on board these fundamentals, you will still need to deal with some of the peripheral issues. This section covers many of those.

HOW TO GET AN ADVISER

You will, no doubt, be assailed from time-to-time by various advisers. You receive unsolicited mail, phone calls and the like. You might even receive invitations to seminars. These should all be treated with a degree of suspicion. All the good advisers I know have more work than they can handle and do not have to go off picking names out of a phone book or share list.

Just as though it were an investment you were planning, you need to sit down and describe the sort of adviser you want. Will this adviser be highly attentive, or rather remote? Do you want somebody with a wide range of qualifications and fewer people skills? Or someone with a great social presence whose technical ability may be less impressive? Obviously you will want the best of all worlds, but it will pay dividends if you sit down and decide the type of adviser that is likely to get on with you. You will know this better than him, or her, so it is only fair that you have an idea to begin with.

You should decide what type of adviser you need and whether or not you need a range. For example, would it be an idea to have one general practitioner, such as an insurance broker, or financial planning consultant who then introduces stockbrokers, solicitors, accountants and so on, as they are required. This is an approach that many people take because there is somebody to share the responsibility.

A good adviser will not be afraid of your cynicism and so if he or she recommends somebody else, then you should ask why and ensure that it is not just a cosy relationship born on the golf course – because it might be!

Finally, you should appreciate the difference between those advisers who act for *you*, and are therefore independent of any institution and those who are paid by a particular institution to act on *its behalf*. The biggest and most obvious area for this is that of insurance people. There are those who are wholly independent and are therefore supposed to recommend products and strategies from a variety of product providers and those that are simply tied to one insurance company and therefore recommend only its products, regardless of whether or not they are the best in the market. You must understand this distinction and you will generally be better served by a good independent adviser.

You will need to decide when you take the adviser on, how he or she is to be remunerated. It is pointless to duck this issue because you need an open and trusting relationship from the start. Generally speaking, you will be far better off paying the individual fees because he or she can then give you wholly independent recommendations without an eye to commission. It should be noted that if an adviser is a bad one and determined to churn you about, then fees may not stop this happening, but it is generally felt that those advisers who have a fee based clientele generally provide a higher standard of ethics and advice.

There is nothing wrong with the commission system, as long as you understand and expect it. An adviser may do a great deal of unpaid work, only then to be 'overpaid' for a particular transaction. However, over the period of a year, things should balance out. The advantage of fees, for both parties, is that you each know where you are and you should know exactly what advice is costing you.

The best way of course to get an adviser is to have one referred to you by your friends. However, do make absolutely sure that they are making a sensible recommendation, otherwise, if they have made some terrible error, you will simply compound it. So, even though the individual is referred to you, put them through the same grilling you would any ordinary adviser. This means asking them for references, sight of their qualifications and proof of their authorisation from the various bodies, such as the Personal Investment Authority or the Securities Association.

You should put a great deal of thought into choosing your adviser because a good one will stay with you for life and will pay his or her remuneration many fold.

PERFORMANCE FIGURES

Many organisations produce performance figures which show their performance to be second to none. However, you should be aware that this information is frequently to be doubted. The reason is that these figures can often be massaged, for example, in terms of the date at which they begin and the date at which the survey finishes. Take the example of a fund which has an appalling history, say, for the years 1991 and 1992. It may then start from a very low base at the beginning of 1993. A new manager may pull the fund round so that, by the end of that year (1993), it is the top performing fund for the year. However, for those people who have been in for the three years, it may still have been a disaster. Such selective performance details are very dangerous. Similarly, it is possible to prove anything by moving other criteria. I know of an organisation that claimed to have the top performing Japanese fund and when I looked into details, they added the riders 'managed by women, from Osaka (not Tokyo) and with a fund size of less than $3m'. There was simply no other fund and hence, no opposition!

You can obtain independent performance figures from Micropal or Hindsight, although these would be expensive and difficult to obtain for individuals. Fortunately, they are re-printed in certain publications, such as Money Management or Pensions Adviser. You should be able to get a pretty good idea of whether or not an organisation can perform over a variety of periods and in a variety of markets. Such magazines may be heavy reading every month, but they occasionally carry priceless surveys, such as The Best Personal Equity Plan, or the Most Flexible TESSA and so on. It is worth, therefore, buying such a publication for three or four pounds every couple of months or so and seeing what is available in the back numbers. On the scale of an investment portfolio and the money that can be lost, such an investment is very small.

COMPUTER PROGRAMMES

It is quite possible these days to get very sophisticated computer programmes which will track your investments and give you an idea of how your portfolio breaks down by sector, or currency. You will be able to get a snapshot of your investment's value by simply pressing a few buttons and whilst the time spent on learning how to use the system is undoubtedly considerable for most people, over the months and years you will reap benefits. You will be able to print out total wealth statements for any adviser you might be meeting and you will be able to consider your needs in several vital areas of investment, for example, pensions or the repayment of your mortgage through PEPs. Generally speaking, running your portfolio on a computer system is a discipline that ensures frequent reviews and a high level of personal attention.

chapter 8

Tax HAVENS

You will have seen throughout the text that tax can be saved by approaching your investment strategy with care. Not only can you reduce the effects of income tax and capital gains tax, which does swell your portfolio and the rate of its growth, but you can even help to avoid or reduce Inheritance Tax when you come to pass on your assets either in your lifetime, or on death.

The example below takes a fairly complicated and artificial example and shows how a married couple might easily reduce the amount of tax they pay very significantly. You may need to read the example several times in order to understand it fully, but, hopefully, the broad principles are clear. You will, of course, need expert advice before you can conclude the detail of your own tax affairs in this way, but it is well worth beginning the exercise now, because on the one hand, your understanding will be greater and on the other hand, any professional whose services you engage should charge less as a result of much of the work having been done.

Example

Tom and Mary have an investment portfolio of £220,000 in Tom's name. They own their home worth £150,000. Tom is a higher rate tax payer and Mary has no income. They have made very basic wills leaving all their estates to one another. They do not 'bed and breakfast' the portfolio.

In 1997 their son needs £50,000 urgently and they sell shares to give it to him. The same year they are both killed in a car accident.

Without planning, their position is as follows:

	£
Portfolio income gross	10,000
Tax at 40 per cent	(4,000)
Net income	6,000
Tax on sale of shares (say)	15,000
Tax on death:	
entire estate	370,000
one exemption	(215,000)
Taxable at 40 per cent	155,000
Tax due	62,000
CGT due	15,000
Net Estate	£293,000

Jack and Jill have the same circumstances except that they have 'bed and breakfasted' their portfolio into PEPs each year and they have transferred it partly to Jill's ownership. All dividends have therefore been tax free, saving some £4,000 of income tax for each of the previous ten years. Their portfolio is therefore worth £290,000. They have made wills with a survivorship clause and have to give their daughter £50,000 in the year of their deaths.

	£
Portfolio income (PEP)	5,000 (tax free)
Portfolio income (non-PEP)	5,000
Mary's allowance	(4,045)
Taxable at 20 per cent	955
Tax	191

Tax on sale of shares Nil because of tax-free PEPs.
Tax on death:

Jack's estate	220,000
Jill's estate	220,000
Nil rate band (x2)	(430,000)
Taxable	10,000
Tax at 40 per cent	(4,000)
Net estate	£436,000
A saving of	£143,000

By the simple act of transferring assets between husband and wife, having an up-to-date will and using personal equity plans, Jack and Jill have been able to leave an extra

£143,000 to their daughter. This is one of the major benefits of tax planning.

You should not just look at the amount you might save in a particular year, but at the way this compounds over time. Further, you have greater flexibility when you have good tax planning. For example, Jack and Jill were able to give their daughter £50,000 at no Inheritance Tax or capital gains tax cost.

While the above example is rather artificial, it could have been made more dramatic by compounding the effect of tax savings over a long period, assuming a higher rate of Inheritance Tax, or assuming greater taxable gains on the portfolio.

ROLL-UP FUNDS

Thousands of people in the UK could benefit immediately from this idea. Anyone with Building Society or Bank deposits can avoid tax altogether on the interest, saving very significant sums over a few years.

Most people have the interest on their capital taxed as it is credited and the net amount paid out to them. However, you can accumulate funds in an off-shore account without paying any tax at all. The first benefit of this is that the account will grow much faster because of compound interest. The second is that by timing your receipt of the funds, you may effectively retain them within your overall affairs, completely tax free. The table below demonstrates how, on reasonable assumptions, the compounding effect over the years becomes greater and greater.

End of Year	Onshore £	Offshore £
1	10,770	11,000
2	11,599	12,100
3	12,492	13,310
4	13,454	14,461
5	14,490	16,105
6	15,606	17,716
7	16,808	19,487
8	18,102	21,436
9	19,496	23,579
10	20,997	25,937

Tax due on roll-up fund £15,937 x 23 per cent = £3,666
Net onshore fund £20,997
Net offshore fund £22,271
Tax free gain £1,274

Of course it may not be convenient for you to hold your money offshore and you could even face a position where tax rates were much higher on repatriating the funds, than they had been during the time of roll-up. But, generally speaking, by obtaining such tax free opportunities, your wealth will increase much faster.

TAX FREE PRODUCTS

By now, you will be able to produce your own projections of how a tax free product or investment can produce a more attractive long-term return and even compensate for charges or occasional lapses in the quality of investment performance.

All individuals should at least consider the following before they construct their investment portfolio:

TESSAs;
PEPs;
National Savings products;
onshore and offshore insurance funds;
roll-up funds;
Unit and Investment trusts;
enterprise investment schemes;
pensions.

PENSIONS

For most people, pensions are rather boring, even though the tax benefits are considerable. On the one hand, there is tax relief on every contribution, whilst on the other hand the funds themselves grow completely free of tax and may well provide a tax free sum on retirement.

However, there are some very sophisticated uses for those people who have sufficient wealth and sufficient nerve to purchase a self-invested personal pension. What this means is that you effectively buy the structure of a pension without the investment management, so no insurance company need be involved. You are then responsible for your own investment management which could be better or worse than that of a life insurance company.

Additionally, the charges are generally fixed and so the more money you have, the smaller they will be as a percentage of your fund. For large funds therefore, there can also be a saving in charges as well as an increase in investment flexibility.

Consider the following example:

73

Tom decides that he will invest £20,000 into a pension scheme in order to play the Stock Market. As you will see from the example, the tax relief immediately boosts his fund so that he starts off with a higher base. By reinvesting gross dividends in the pension scheme and avoiding capital gains tax altogether – because pension funds are tax free – he ends up with an improvement of £96,000 over a personal holding. Whilst there is a great deal of inflexibility surrounding pensions, increasing your return by over 78 per cent must be attractive.

	Self-invested Personal Holding £	Pension £
Initial investment	20,000	26,000
ten year result, dividends reinvested, CGT paid	122,000	218,000
Increase in pension scheme ie + 78 per cent		£96,000

Of course, the smart investor places those assets with the likelihood of most dramatic capital appreciation in his pension scheme. As property is a legitimate investment, it would be quite possible to buy commercial land within your pension scheme which might then be developed, turning its value from thousands of pounds into millions. With a personal pension scheme, there is no limit on the benefits you may take and you could find that the tax free cash portion of the fund would be a multiple of the figure with which you started, so that any residual pension is truly free.

CHANGING PEOPLE'S WILLS

It is not possible to consider all the various methods of reducing Inheritance Tax, but one is very attractive. It concerns the alteration of somebody's will when they have already died. For example, in the example of Tom and Mary above, Inheritance Tax is paid because there is no survivorship clause in the will. The whole of Tom and Mary's estates are bunched together because Tom is deemed to have died before Mary by virtue of being older, even though they may have died simultaneously in the same accident. If they had a survivorship clause in the will, each of them would have a nil rate band of £215,000 to play with and they would have paid no Inheritance Tax at all. This simple measure would have saved them £86,000 in tax! Unfortunately, they were too silly to make such a will. The good news, however, is that within two years of their deaths and subject to the consent of all the beneficiaries, the will can be altered so that the survivorship clause is inserted. In this way, you can change the destination of property from any individual to any other individual, which can be particularly tax efficient.

One popular use of this 'deed of variation', is when a couple die, leaving their estate to their own children who are already wealthy. They vary the will so that the legacy passes down to the deceased's grandchildren, thus skipping a generation for Inheritance Tax.

Incidentally, you cannot use these clever devices if you have not made a will in the first place! So, that has to be the first step.

chapter 9

The golden RULES

I have tried to extract from the diverse and confusing world of investment, several key principles; the real return, the net return to you and the clear definition of your aims, being three cornerstones. What this section does is give you certain rules to which you can refer from time-to-time to check whether or not you are on track. If you stick to these rules, along with the fundamentals of investment, you should not go far wrong and should achieve a return in excess of that which you might otherwise have achieved:

1   The first rule is always start with *you* − define your aims clearly, objectively and stick to them;

2 Never let taxation dictate your investment policy –
   take it into account, but do not be led entirely by it;
3 Carry out frequent reviews of your investments – your
   policy might be suitable at the outset, but circumstances might change. Quarterly valuations are generally worthwhile, whilst those of you with more active
   investment might review things more frequently;
4 Cut your losses when you have to – set limits for
   both profits and losses and when you reach those
   limits, unless things have changed fundamentally,
   you should bale out one way or another;
5 Make sure you always use all your tax allowances –
   if you can do so without cramping your overall
   investment policy;
6 Remember, the net return is important – you should
   enhance it in whatever way possible;
7 Do not be afraid to use your own judgement – your
   instincts can be a valuable safeguard;
8 Concentrate on value for money, not the absolute
   cost – it is better to pay 1.5 per cent for successful
   investment management than 1 per cent for a failure;
9 Don't risk money that you cannot afford to lose –
   make sure your risk profile matches your psycho-
   logical needs as well as your financial needs;
10 Only ever deal with fully authorised intermediaries.

Appendix A

USEFUL ORGANISATIONS

The following addresses may be useful:

The Banking Ombudsman
70 Grays Inn Road
LONDON WC1X 8NB
Tel: 0171 404 9944
Fax: 0171 405 5052

The Building Society Ombudsman
Grosvenor Gardens House, 35/37 Grosvenor Gardens
LONDON SW1X 7AW
Tel: 0171 931 0044
Fax: 0171 931 8485

The Insurance Ombudsman
Citygate 1, 135 Park Street
LONDON SE1 9EA
Tel: 0171 928 7600
Fax: 0171 401 8700

The Investment Ombudsman
IMRO, Broadwalk House, 6 Apple Street
LONDON EC2A 2AA
Tel: 0171 628 6022
Fax: 0171 920 9285

The PIA Ombudsman
1 London Wall
LONDON EC2Y 5EA
Tel: 0181 600 3838
Fax: 0171 600 4727

The Personal Investment Authority
Hertsmere House, Hertsmere Road
LONDON E14 4AB
Tel: 0171 538 8860
Fax: 0171 895 8579

The Securities and Investment Board
Gavrell House, 2/14 Bunhill Row
LONDON EC1Y 8RA
Tel: 0171 638 1240
Fax: 0171 382 5900

The Institute of Financial Planning
Hereford House, East Street
HEREFORD HR1 2LU
Tel: 01432 274891

Appendix B

INVESTMENT MATRIX

INVESTMENT TYPE	NIL	INCOME TAX BASIC	HIGHER	CAPITAL GAINS TAX
CASH	Reclaim	No further	Further	No Tax
NATIONAL SAVINGS ACCOUNT	No Tax	No Tax	No Tax	No Tax
NATIONAL SAVINGS INC. BONDS	No Tax	Basic Rate to pay	Basic and higher to pay	No Tax
GILTS/ CORPORATE BONDS	Reclaim	No Further	Further	No Tax

NATIONAL SAVINGS CERTIFICATES	No Tax	No Tax	No Tax	No Tax
SHARES	Reclaim	No Further	Further	Yes
UNIT TRUSTS	Reclaim	No Further	Further	Yes
INVESTMENT TRUSTS	Reclaim	No Further	Further	Yes
INSURANCE BONDS	No Tax No Reclaim	No Tax	Further	No Tax
OFFSHORE INSURANCE BONDS	No Tax	Basic Rate to pay	Basic and higher to pay	No Tax
PERSONAL EQUITY PLANS	No Tax	No Tax	No Tax	No Tax
VENTURE CAPITAL TRUSTS	No Tax	No Tax	No Tax	No Tax
OFFSHORE ROLL-UP FUNDS	No Tax	Basic rate to pay	Basic and higher to pay	No Tax
PURCHASED LIFE ANNUITIES	Reclaim	Basic rate to pay	Further	No Tax
PENSION INCOME	Reclaim	No Further	Further	No Tax
2ND HAND LIFE POLICIES	No Tax	No Tax	No Tax	Yes
QUALIFYING LIFE POLICIES	No Tax	No Tax	No Tax	No Tax
GUARANTEED INCOME BONDS	No Tax	No Further	Further	No Tax

Appendix C

RISK PROFILE

WHAT IS YOUR RISK PROFILE?	{ **LOW** – USE THE { BLUE CHART { { **MEDIUM** – USE THE { GREEN CHART { { **HIGH** – USE THE { RED CHART

THE BLUE CHART

NIL	Consider Cash*	Gilts		With profit policies		With profit policies
24%	Consider TESSA*	Gilts	NSCs	With profit policies	Guaranteed bonds	
40%	Consider TESSA*	Low yielding Gilts	NSCs	Guaranteed Bonds	Guaranteed PEPs	With profit policies

THE GREEN CHART

NIL	Consider Cash*	Gilts	Corporate bonds	Non-specialist Unit Trusts	Guaranteed equity funds/Trackers	
24%	Consider TESSA*	General PEPs*	Gilts	Unit-linked policies*	Non-specialist Unit Trusts*	Guaranteed equity fund/Trackers
40%	Consider TESSA*	General PEPs*	NSCs	Unit-linked policies*	Non-specialist Unit Trusts*	Guaranteed equity fund/Trackers

* Indicates regular saving available

THE RED CHART

NIL	Consider Cash*	General and single co PEP	Individual equities	Specialist* unit and Investment Trusts	Woodlands options
24%	Consider TESSA*	General and single co PEP	EIS	Individual equities	Specialist* unit and Investment Trusts
40%	Consider TESSA*	General and single co PEP	VCTs/EIS	Individual equities	Specialist fund insurance bonds*

* Indicates regular saving available

Appendix A

TRADING STRATEGIES

𝒜t is quite possible to trade in Derivatives and control your risk rather than exposing yourself to the unquantified losses which might occur.

Many people consider the 'buy write' strategy to be a very easy way to make money. An investor buys a share as well as an option on that share. For example, imagine that Natwest Bank shares are £9.00 each. You invest £900 in the shares and at the same time you will invest £100 in a call option or a put option in those shares. If the price collapses you can exercise your put option to make profits and then re-invest in the share at the collapsed price. If alternatively, the price rises sharply you have the profit from the rise in the stock and the geared rise on the option. Of course, if there is no major price movement either way then the amount you paid for the option will be lost.

As an alternative you can invest all your funds in Natwest Bank shares at £9.00 and then write an option on them. Imagine you write the option with an exercise price of £10 and you get an option premium of £1. If the share price rises but not to £10 you will not be exercised. You will keep all the share price rises as well as the option premium. So if the share price rise were 90p in this example, you would in fact have doubled the growth on the shares that would have been available to an investor not using options. As long as the share rises, the option premium is effectively free money. If the share price goes up beyond the exercise price and you are exercised, then you will have to sell the shares at £10 and keep the option premium, making £2 on your original £9. As long as the expiry date of the option is not too close, say three or six months, then you will be entirely happy, because you have made £2 on £9, in only three or six months.

As long as you choose your exercise price carefully, being a price at which you would in any case have sold the shares, then the option premium is always free money. A great many institutional fund managers use this tactic and even though they will be caught out if the share rises to, say, £13 and they are forced to sell at £10, the fact of having received so many option premiums when the market is not rising sharply, generally works out for them.

As usual, the most dire of warnings must be added to any section on options trading!

Appendix E

TRADING

If you carry out an activity repeatedly, or have transactions which are very unusual and cannot easily be explained as a hobby or a one-off, then the Inland Revenue may decide that you are trading. Of course, this needn't be a problem because once you are trading you fall into the income tax regime rather than the capital gains tax regime. Accordingly, you can offset certain expenses and fund a pension from your profits. In many cases individuals have actively tried to be deemed to be trading rather than making capital gains.

The Criteria which the Inland Revenue apply are varied. Firstly, they look at the subject matter of any asset which you have bought and sold. If it is say, a painting or second home, then it is the type of asset which people regularly do buy as an investment. However, if it were say, six tonnes of fruit, then it would be unlikely that you have bought this for any other reason than selling it on. So the type of asset in question can point towards trading. Similarly, your length of ownership can also be a factor. Clearly, if you were to buy a collection of stamps and hold them for five years before re-sale, this would hardly be trading. But, turning over your portfolio of stamps every few weeks would indicate a trading activity. The frequency with which you carry out the transactions can also be relevant. For example, an individual who changes his car every year is unlikely to be trading, but changing it every week is another story.

Finally, your motives in buying and selling the asset in the first place need to be examined. For example, candlesticks or a piano are the sort of thing you might have in your living room. You might like to start playing the piano or you might simply like to smarten up your living space. However, if you were to buy a piano knowing that you have pre-sold it, then surely your only motive could be profit rather than enjoyment of the asset itself.

So in general you need to be very careful when you deal in capital assets and make sure that you know whether or not you will be deemed to be trading.

Glossary

AGE ALLOWANCE	– An increased personal allowance for those people aged over 65 at the beginning of the tax year.
ANTI-AVOIDANCE	– Special tax legislation to combat tax avoidance schemes.
AVERAGING	– Sometimes a phased investment will average out the price at which shares or units are bought.
AVOIDANCE	– The use of legitimate means to reduce your tax bill.
BEAR MARKET	– This is a depressed market where prices are moving downwards.
BED AND BREAKFAST	A system of selling and imme- – diately re-acquiring assets in

order to realise a chargeable gain or allowable loss.

BONUS ISSUES — New shares issued to existing shareholders increasing the number they hold, but possibly decreasing the price accordingly.

BUDGET — The annual presentation to the House of Commons by the Chancellor of changes in fiscal policy.

BULL MARKET — A market where prices are generally moving upwards.

BUSINESS EXPANSION SCHEME — An investment on which full tax relief was available, the proceeds being entirely free of tax after a five-year qualifying period.

CGT — Capital gains tax.

CHARGEABLE GAINS — Gains you make which are possibly liable to capital gains tax.

CTT — Capital-transfer tax.

DERIVATIVES — Generally complicated investment mechanisms to gear up, or down, the effect of price movements in underlying securities.

ESTATE — The total of your world-wide property.

EVASION — The use of illegal methods to avoid paying tax.

INDEPENDENT ADVISER — One who is not tied to any insurance company, investment institution or bank and should therefore make independent recommendations.

INDEPENDENT
TAXATION — A system whereby a husband and wife can be treated as entirely separate individuals for income tax and capital gains tax purposes.

INDEXATION
ALLOWANCE — A means of allowing for inflation on chargeable gains, so that only the true gain is taxed.

INHERITANCE
TAX — The tax on the value of your estate on death or certain gifts when made during your lifetime.

INTESTATE — One who dies without having made a valid will.

PERSONAL
ALLOWANCES — A set level of deduction from income before income tax is applied.

PERSONAL
EQUITY PLAN
(PEP) — A mechanism for the holding of shares or unit trusts on which there will be no income tax or capital gains tax.

REAL RETURN — The actual rate of return in excess of the prevailing rate of inflation.

RISK BANDING — The practice of building up a variety of different investments with differing risk profiles to achieve an overall effect.

ROLL-UP FUND — An off-shore based investment where the interest content is accumulated year-on-year without crystallising your tax liability until sold.

TAX PAYERS CHARTER	A statement of Inland Revenue – policy as to how they deal with the public.
TESSA	– Tax Exempt Special Savings Arrangement, whereby the income from a deposit account may be credited without income tax deductions, subject to a five-year holding period.
TIED AGENT	– An individual who acts on behalf of only one insurance company or investment institution and does not therefore give independent advice.
TRUST	– A mechanism whereby one party (the Trustee), holds assets for another party (the Beneficiary), usually at the request of the Settlor (the one who introduced the assets in the first place).
WIDOW'S BEREAVEMENT ALLOWANCE	A specific allowance which may be claimed by a widow in the – year of her husband's death and the following year.
YEAR OF ASSESSMENT	The tax year which runs from – April 6th through to April 5th.

Index

Numbers in italics refer to glossary definitions